MILF THE MUSICAL

#MOTHER #INFLUENCER #LIKE #FOLLOW

Created by Sally Knight
Written by Sally Knight & Jennifer Francis
Music by Sally Knight, Hugo Perricone & Bligh Water
Lyrics by Sally Knight

ORiGiN™
Theatrical

FOR ALL ENQUIRIES CONTACT:
ORiGiN™ Theatrical
PO BOX Q1235, QVB Post Office, Sydney, NSW, 1230, Australia
Phone: (61 2) 8514 5201
enquiries@originmusic.com.au   www.origintheatrical.com.au
Part of the ORiGiN™ Music Group
An Australian Independent Music Company

IMPORTANT NOTICE

USE OF COPYRIGHTED MUSIC

music licensing authority in your territory for the rights to any incidental music. In Australia and New Zealand, contact APRA AMCOS apraamcos.com.au.

IMPORTANT BILLING AND CREDIT REQUIREMENTS

If you obtained performance rights to perform this title, please refer to your licensing agreement for important billing and credit requirements.

If you are in any doubt about any of the above then contact ORiGiN™ Theatrical.

For complete listing of plays and musicals available to perform and all licence enquiries, contact ORiGiN™ Theatrical.

CHARACTERS

KATE - vivacious mother and fashion influencer in her early- mid 40s. Strong singing and acting role with some dancing.

CLEO - Kate's glamorous younger sister, around 40. Strong singing and dancing role.

JASON - Kate's husband, advertising executive, mid 40s. Strong singing and dancing role. (Also play BRAD, the young traveller)

FRANKIE - Kate's BFF, a successful drag queen and night club owner, mid 40s. Strong singing role with some dancing.

STARDUST - Frankie's off-sider in the Drag show, mid-late 20s. Strong singing and dancing role. (Also play SECURITY GUARD)

BANJO - Acapulco Waitress and Cleo's new love interest, 20- 40s. Swing/Ensemble singer and strong dancer (Also play HOT WAITER and PAPARRAZZI)

GLORIA - Kate's mother, 60s, strong acting, cameo role. On screen appearance only.

NANNA - Kate's grandmother, 80s. Strong acting, cameo role. On screen appearance only.

THE GUY - small cameo (potentially famous face), 50-60's, on screen only.

All roles should have good comic timing.

POSSIBLE ENSEMBLE & DANCERS - eg Brad/Security Guard/ Hot Waiter/Paparazzi/Banjo; Red carpet celebrities & photographers, Internet people (She Said), Frankie's club patrons and performers, Acapulco club patrons, Acapulco show extras.

MUSICAL NUMBERS

MILF (KATE, ENSEMBLE & PAPARAZZI)

MILFING IT FOR ALL ITS WORTH (KATE & ENSEMBLE)

I LOVE YOUR WAY (JASON & KATE)

LOUD (KATE & JASON)

SHE SAID (CLEO & ENSEMBLE)

DANCE (FRANKIE & STARDUST)

PENNED WITH INK (FRANKIE & JASON)

HOLIDAY (KATE & CLEO)

MIDLIFE CRISIS (STARDUST, FRANKIE, CLEO & KATE)

SPOONFULL (CLEO, KATE & ENSEMBLE)

WOMAN (KATE)

STAY (KATE)

THE BOMB (JASON)

CHERRY SUNDAY (KATE & CLEO)

MY SONG (KATE)

STRONGER STRONGER (FRANKIE, KATE & WHOLE CAST)

SCENE ONE - THE RED CARPET

Series of Social Media Posts from FashionEsther (Kate's alter-ego), appears on screen.

Cinderella YES Pumpkin NO. Orange is not the new black @shabarra #fashioncrimes

Faux-fur or road kill @francissalsbury? #shalloween #hauntedcouture

Dog-chew-toy clutch a nice touch @fardi #houndstooth

Tippi inspo? Feathered fascinator or did The Birds attack @gicci? #nestingonyourlaurels #hitchcock

Salivating for Salisbury's spring release @francissalsbury. Got to be better than last year's red on red #menstrualmonstrosity

Music. Glamorous fashion opening with cameras flashing. On screen vision of celebrities and paparazzi. Screen reveals

"Francis Salsbury Spring Show"

A wall of yellow smoke, KATE enters as alter ego influencer FashionEsther, wearing pink dress taking a selfie (as per logo).

FRANKIE close behind, she hands him the phone and he films.

PAPPARAZZI excited and react, as FashionEsther draws all the attention with her signature entrance. Paparazzi snaps shots while she sings. Frankie videos while FashionEsther tries to mingle with CELEBRITIES.

SONG: MILF

KATE (singing)
Here I am at the show
All the cameras flash! Click!
Showing off my "best" side

Applying my best lipstick
Faking it, making it
And with a little luck
I can be the online mother
That you'd like to fuh-uh-ollow

KATE AND ENSEMBLE
Follow

TINA PAPPARAZZI
FashionEsther! Over here! (take pic) Surprised to see you here
tonight. Didn't think you'd be Salsbury's favourite person after that
review!

KATE
Just telling it like it is, Tina. How's Tommy and the kids?

TINA PAPPARAZZI
You've just cracked 2,000,000 followers.
What's your secret?

KATE
I'm real. I'm a mother, influencer... like me? Follow!

Paparazzi smiles and starts to work on phone.

KATE
I don't wanna be bitchy
But if it's itchy
I'm gonna tell the truth

If it's faulty or if it's flawed
I'm sharing that with the world
I'm gonna tell the truth

The paparazzi's story appears on the screen.

"FashionEsther - self-proclaimed MILF - mother, influencer, like, follow".

Kate is initially shocked but decides to run with it.

KATE
I'm FashionEsther and I can see
Nobody's gonna put that shit on me
I'm a MILF and I know my own style
I know my body and I know my mind
I'm a MILF, M-I-L-F
But I never said that I was per-er- er-fect

ENSEMBLE
She's a MILF, M-I-L-F
But she never said that she was
per-er-er-fect

KATE
When I get to posting
I just cannot stop the flow
I just can't wait to say
Everything I know
Dinner burning, house a mess
Kids all run a muck
But I could be the online mother
That you'd like to fuh-uh-ollow

ENSEMBLE
Follow

KATE
Follow

ENSEMBLE

Follow

KATE
If blue is the new black
But it makes you feel like crap
I'm gonna tell the truth

If shoulder pads make a comeback
Looking like a quarterback
I'm gonna tell the truth

I'm FashionEsther and I can see
Nobody's gonna put that shit on me
I'm a MILF and I know my own style
I know my body and I know my mind
I'll tell it straight
Like there's no tomorrow
Cause I am the mother
You'd like to fuh-uh-ollow –
(with ensemble)
I'm a MILF
M-I-L-F
But I never said that I was perfect

KATE
I'm a MILF M-I-L-F
But I never said that I was perfect

ENSEMBLE
No she never said that she was perfect
No she never said that she was perfect
No she never said that she was perfect

END SONG

Music changes – Kate tries to enter the show, but she has no ticket. SECURITY GUARD stops her, she tries to push her way through.

TINA PAPPARAZZI
So, FashionEsther, is being a MILF worth it?

Kate scuffles with the guard until he slaps handcuffs on her and everyone freezes, Kate in shock.

Yellow smoke bursts forth again. Kate walks forward again through the smoke to sing. Ensemble is frozen until chorus when they all begin to dance along with her.

SONG: MILFING IT FOR ALL ITS WORTH

KATE
Fashion designer when I was young
Time flies now a wife, a mum
I started posting liking and such
Seems like the meaner I was, the more likes I got
Say what you like, if I post that I'm dead
I read your responses and left 'em read
With every truth and line I tweet I'm hotter than hot!
Like a dog on heat.

Cause I'm Milfing it for all it's worth
I'm Milfing it
Haven't you heard
I'm Milfing it
For all its worth

ENSEMBLE
She's Milfing it, Milfing it, Milfing it, Milfing it

KATE

For all it's worth.

END SONG

Blackout.

SCENE CHANGE – ON SCREEN Social media posts from
FashionEsther (note, Kate is FashionEsther in all pics):

Mugshot mayhem #milf #getoutofmylight

From Chanel to shackles #brassbracelets #milf

Rather be arrested than watching Salisbury's #crimesoffashion #milf

SCENE TWO – KATE & JASON'S BEDROOM, LATER THAT NIGHT

Kate and Jason enter their bedroom, in a steamy embrace.

KATE

Mmmm, Jason! Maybe I should get arrested more often.

JASON

Shame they didn't let us keep the handcuffs.

KATE

Oh, didn't they?

She pulls a set of handcuffs from her handbag.

JASON

Oh Kate, I love your way.

SONG: I LOVE YOUR WAY

JASON (Singing)
You're so cool
You know that I am your fool
And that's alright
And that's alright
You knock me offa my feet
Whenever we meet
It's outta sight
It's outta sight
You know I'd jump in your queue
You know I'd do it for you
I'll play if you want me to play

KATE AND JASON
Baby Baby Baby Baby I love your way
Baby Baby Baby Baby I love your way

KATE
Ooooooo
I think about you all of the time
I feel I'm losin' my mind
You could have me every other day
Just call me when you're ready to play

KATE AND JASON
Baby Baby Baby Baby I love your way
Baby Baby Baby Baby I love your way

DANCE BREAK

END SONG

Jason handcuffs one of her wrists to the bed.

                    JASON
          Who's been a naughty girl?

                    KATE
          But Salsbury's Spring release. I had to be there. I wasn't going to
          let a little thing like the lack of an invitation stop me. It's all about
          being on top of my game.

Her phone is pinging madly.

                    KATE
          See? My public need me.

Jason is slowly getting onto the bed on top of Kate, but she's distracted
now by the phone.

                    JASON
          Speaking of being on top of your game.

She reaches over to the phone and picks it up, tipping Jason off.

                    JASON
          Not on top of my game then.

                    KATE
          Oh, of course, sorry. I'm just muting it, see?

They continue to make out, but Kate doesn't actually put down the
phone. She's looking over Jason's shoulder at the screen.

KATE

Oh my god, oh my god

JASON

Yes, yes

KATE

Oh my god! Frankie!

Jason pauses abruptly. He stops and looks at Kate.

JASON

What?

KATE

The red carpet video is blowing up. We're viral!

JASON

We? You were arrested, Kate.

KATE

Oh right, it's just me now is it? Even though WE had babies, and
WE make dinner, and WE crashed the car
- no WE this time?
Anyway, technically, FashionEsther was arrested.

JASON

Yeah well FashionEsther needs some serious therapy.

KATE

A minute ago you thought it was hot.

JASON

Yeah, and then you called me Frankie.

KATE

Oh, don't be so melodramatic.

Jason undoes the cuff on the bedhead. Kate gets up on the other side of the bed. They are both angry.

KATE

You're just jealous because I'm the one getting the attention. I've supported your career for years.

JASON

My job is 9-5. But FashionEsther is 24/7.

KATE

You just want a good little wife quiet in the background.

JASON

Ha - Quiet? With only a million people waiting to hear what you think?

SONG: LOUD

KATE

I know on paper you're perfect
I know possessions you've earned it
And I think you can't see the sky for the clouds.

JASON

I say, then you say it's different
Then you say it's black when it's blue
And you think you're always holding the cards
Why you gotta be so loud?
Why you gotta be so loud?

You're drowning me out

KATE AND JASON
You're drowning me out

KATE
You say be true to yourself
It's not easy being a MILF
I just want my voice, my voice to be heard

JASON
For crying out loud.
Why you gotta be so loud?

KATE AND JASON
Why you gotta to be so loud
You're drowning me out
You're drowning me out

KATE
I have a life outside

JASON
Just want you by my side

KATE
I can't always just be the wife at your side

JASON
No, because you're always online
You're always online

KATE
Not all the time
(Kate trails off as she is looking at her phone)

JASON

Yes all the time
You never ever think twice

KATE

You say that because you're a louse

JASON

Just want you by my side

KATE

Not all the time
All the time

JASON

Is that such a crime?
Is that such a crime?

KATE

Why does this have to be so hard
Drowning each other out
It might be we're both just too proud all the time

JASON

Could it be that we don't belong
Seems like we've sung this song before

KATE

Before
Why does this have to be so hard

KATE AND JASON

Drowning each other out
It might be we're both just too proud all the time
All the time

END SONG

CLEO bursts into the bedroom. She pauses and looks at Kate and Jason, Kate wearing the handcuffs.

> CLEO
>
> My life is over. I'm leaving Richard. I know you always called him Dr. Dick and now I know why. And my boobs are so sore and I need wine.

Jason looks at Cleo, then Kate.

> JASON
>
> Loud.

Jason heads for the door.

> KATE
>
> Jason!

Jason looks back and Kate blows him a hopeful kiss. He catches it in mid-air, throws it on the ground and stomps on it. Jason exits.

> CLEO
>
> Were you guys in the middle of something?

> KATE
>
> You think? What's up, Cleo?

> CLEO
>
> Sorry, sorry, I should have called
> – I'll go.

KATE

No, no, no. What do you need?

CLEO

Give me your phone, I'll show you. What's your password? Hang on, birthday. Gawd, you're so old.

KATE

Shut up.

Cleo opens FacePage, it can be seen on the screen. She goes to Richard's profile, looks in his Friends list, finds The Girl, and goes to her profile. There's a very recent photo of Richard and the Girl together. She scrolls to the comments on the pic, and reads them aloud.

CLEO

Gorgeous couple! You guys are always so much fun!

She drops the phone.

CLEO

Everyone knows.

SONG: SHE SAID

CLEO *(singing)*
She said that he's been round a few times,
She said that he's been telling me lies,
She said that he's been at her side,
She said that it's been more than one night.

His boots been under another bed,
Another pillow been resting his head,

He says he's working late earning more bread,
That's what he said, what he said, what he said.

She said that he's been driving her wild
She said that he's been there night after night.
She said come the morning light. I'm still none the wiser.

ENSEMBLE

She said, I said, he said, you said, they said, this said, think you
better stop said.
They said, you said, why said, can't said, this said, who said, think
you better change said.

She said, I said, he said, we said, they said, he said, think you better
stop said.

They said, you said, why said, can't said, him said, instead think we
better change said.

CLEO

When was he going to tell me,
Did it enter his head,
Now I'm hurt and angry all because of what she said,
Doesn't mind what he does
Doesn't mind what he says,
Didn't have the guts to tell me
Are these the games he plays?

I told him last time,
Things between us had to change,
Now I'm out of my mind,
'Cause he's with her, with her
instead, instead, instead, instead

Oh, she said that he's been driving her wild,

She said that he's been there night after night,
She said come the morning light,
I'm still none the wiser.

ENSEMBLE
She said, I said, he said, you said, they said, this said, think you
better stop said.

They said, you said, why said, can't said, this said, who said, think
you better change said.
She said, I said, he said, we said, they said, he said, think you better
stop said they said.

You said, why said, can't said, him said, instead think you better
change said.

Enter his head
Doesn't mind what he does
Doesn't mind what he says

END SONG

KATE
Well who listens to what anyone says online right?

Cleo gives her a look. Then throws the phone.

KATE
Yeah sister! Hang on, that's my phone.

Kate retrieves the phone. Cleo begins to cry.

KATE

You can stay here as long as you want. The kids too. Jason will be fine with it. I'm sure.

On Kate's phone, Facechat call from Gloria, Kate and Cleo's mother.

KATE

It's mum.

CLEO

Don't tell her I'm here.

Kate answers the video call, falsely cheerful.

KATE

Hi Ma!

GLORIA

Arrested! I saw that Esther fiasco. How's jail? Your poor father would be turning in his grave. (crosses self) They say any publicity is good publicity … I mean it wouldn't be my cup of tea but far be it from me to tell you how to live your life.

KATE

Jason bailed me out.

Cleo, unaware of events, is now piecing things together.

CLEO

Oh, the handcuffs.

GLORIA

Is that Cleo?

CLEO
Hi Ma.

GLORIA
Look girls, I'm in a bit of a pickle. I swiped right and well, David, he's lovely, but my god it's after 1am Kate and he just keeps wanting to talk and dance and buy me cocktails. I'm exhausted. I'm on the lam, in the toilets. Kate, I need to you to call me "from jail" and say you need me to bail you out.

KATE
Can't you just say you're tired?

GLORIA
I don't want him to think I'm old.

CLEO
I get that.

KATE
You'd rather tell your date your daughter's in prison, than admit that you're old and tired and want to go home.

The door opens. Frankie enters excitedly, followed slowly by Jason who's holding a glass and bottle of wine.

FRANKIE
Kate, darling, the whole MILF thing! It's genius. We're viral!

They hug and clap excitedly. Jason is not impressed.

JASON
Really?

CLEO

MILF? Kate? Um hello? (Gestures to herself. Takes the wine bottle from Jason and swigs. She nods at Frankie) Frankenstein.

FRANKIE

Cleopatra! Haven't seen you without bandages in a while.

CLEO

Well not that you can see (touches her sore chest). But I still look 20.

FRANKIE

I would too if I had your Dick. We can't all be married to plastic surgeons.

CLEO

Well, now my Dick is CUT OFF!

FRANKIE

Need to get something off your chest, beside those bandages?

CLEO

It's so cliche its embarrassing. He's banging the Nanny. She's so young, she thinks the Berlin Wall is a boy band.

FRANKIE

Bastard!

JASON

Dr DICK.

GLORIA

Oh Cleo, I'm sorry to hear that. Are you sure?

CLEO

She's sharing the love all over her and his socials. Like I wouldn't see it.

FRANKIE

No! After all the work he's put into you! Even you don't deserve that.

CLEO

Meanwhile, you look fabulous... (she gasps in realization) You've been seeing Doctor Dick!

FRANKIE

What? I'm a hairy man in a dress! I hate Dick, but I need Dick more than you do! I've got Stardust stealing my spotlight every chance he gets, with his perky little pecs and nubile flexibility -

KATE

- and those tight little butt cheeks...Sorry.

JASON

So Cleo, are you staying here? I mean it's fine.

CLEO

Are you serious? Richard's the one who can slum it. He can have the beach house. But I'm going to stand on my own two feet. I'm going to get a job.

Pause, then everybody laughs, including Cleo.

CLEO

No, really, I've got to look after myself. I'll go back to my roots.

FRANKIE

Ooh, that's a very long list.

CLEO

There wasn't that many.

They pause, then all burst out into laughter again.

CLEO

I meant, dance teaching.

KATE

You could use Frankie's studio!

FRANKIE

Come to the club tomorrow night. I want you all to see the new number anyway. (hugs Kate and notices the handcuffs). Kinky! I like it. (hugs Jason) Lemonade out of Lemons. Nice one.

Frankie exits.

GLORIA

Meanwhile, I'm still in the bathroom.

CLEO

I'll take care of it. I'm going to bed. Mum, I'll give you five to get back to the table.

GLORIA

Lovely. Bye everyone! Now, Cleo, speaking of roots (she leans in close and taps her hairline, and hangs up)

Cleo, annoyed, hands Kate the phone.

CLEO

She's on her own.

Cleo exits.

Kate and Jason are left alone. It's awkward.

KATE

Could be nice to hang out at the club together? A bit of a dance, a couple of drinks? The kids can go to mums.

JASON

About that. I've got a client meeting, then dinner.

KATE

Of course. With your 9 to 5 job.

Jason sculls his wine, grabs his pillow off the bed and exits.

END SCENE - BLACKOUT

SCENE CHANGE - ON SCREEN Social media posts from FashionEsther:

Got Sprung @francissalsbury #milf #fashionfugitive

Feeling the love – thanks Esties! #milf #fashionfreedom

Mad for drag #feathers #fabulousfrankie

SCENE THREE - FRANKIE'S NIGHTCLUB, NEXT EVENING

Music. Retro nightclub with a stage and 70's dance floor.

Screen shows nightclub/crowd etc. HOT WAITER enters (bumless chaps) and dances/serving drinks.

Enter Stardust in full drag to do intro dance. Kate and Cleo enter, move to a table together to watch the show. Frankie enters in full drag to perform.

During the song, Stardust has some wardrobe issues and becomes frustrated.

SONG: DANCE

FRANKIE

I heard it was the place to go,
Music soft and low,
I saw your eyes looking over me
I suddenly felt alone,
The music way down low,
Electric lights came down and there you were in front of me

FRANKIE AND STARDUST

Dance
You said dance
You said dance
You said dance

We danced around the floor
We danced a little more
We danced, we danced, we danced, we danced

FRANKIE

We danced into the night,
The stars were burning bright,
Your lips pressed against mine,
And then we danced some more

Your eyes locked on mine,

And we were moving in time,
I felt your hands caress
all around my soul

FRANKIE AND STARDUST

You said dance
You said dance
You said dance
You said dance

We danced around the floor,
We danced a little more,
We danced, we danced, we danced, we danced

We danced

You said dance
You said dance
You said dance
You said dance
We danced around the floor,
We danced a little more,
We danced, we danced, we danced, we danced

We danced

END SONG

Frankie makes his way to where Cleo and Kate are sitting/standing. Stardust exits in a huff holding his costume together.

FRANKIE
After all these years, I still get a rush from performing.

CLEO

Maybe you should have that looked at. Now, play host and get us a drink please, Frankenstein.

FRANKIE
Speaking of hosts - how's the STD?

CLEO
Ask your boyfriend - he gave it to me.

FRANKIE
Ah Cleopatra, you're almost fun. You definitely need a drink.

CLEO
Thank you, I did just have to watch your show - you should probably get one for everyone in here.

Frankie motions to the HOT WAITER who comes over.

FRANKIE
Cherry Sundaes for them, and two orgasms for me.

Stardust arrives at their table, wearing a glam dressing gown, costume in hand.

STARDUST
Frankie. These costumes are falling apart. They're as old as... (looks suggestively at Frankie). Kate! Can't you do something?

KATE
Stardust, you are looking really hot tonight! Have you lost weight?

STARDUST
Yes, not that anybody noticed (looks at Frankie) - I have been

trying...

FRANKIE

Speaking of costuming. Kate, I wanted to ask you a favour.

KATE

Of course, Frankie. Anything.

FRANKIE

The Guy called me this morning. The Acapulco gig is a go!

STARDUST

Acapulco?

KATE

That's brilliant, Frankie! And the Guy will be there?

STARDUST

The guy?

FRANKIE

That's the deal!

KATE

Frankie that's amazing! He's going to love you. He'll see
straight away that you're perfect! (to Cleo) This Producer Guy is
considering Frankie to host a net series being shot in Acapulco.
(to Frankie) So what happens now?

STARDUST

Who's the guy?

FRANKIE

He wants to see me perform live. He's arranged a short run at
Crystal Queer in Acapulco. Neon everywhere. Neon on me. And

I need all new costuming to knock this thing out of the park, my darling Kate.

                    KATE
I'll get started straight away.

                    STARDUST
We're going to Acapulco?

                    FRANKIE
I'm going to Acapulco. My knees can't do this every night for the rest of my life.

                    STARDUST
You're leaving me behind?

                    FRANKIE
Don't pretend you won't love having this spotlight all to yourself.

                    STARDUST
But what about our perfect double act? What about us?

                    FRANKIE
You'll simply have to do it alone.

Stardust exit. Hot Waiter arrives with drinks.

                    FRANKIE
Oooh, Orgasms!

As the Hot Waiter turns to go Frankie notices the bare bum cheeks (Waiter's wearing chaps with a g-string).

FRANKIE

That reminds me - I need to pop to the bakery on the way home.

CLEO

More importantly, I need to look at this studio space.

FRANKIE

Right now? Fine... (to Kate) Sit tight, we'll be back in a jiffy. Here, these will keep you company.

He hands his drink to Kate.

KATE

I can't have two orgasms!

FRANKIE

Poor you.

Frankie and Cleo exit. Kate sits alone at the table, sipping her drinks. She gets her phone out and texts Jason. The conversation appears on screen.

KATE: *You should be here! Frankie gave me two orgasms already*

JASON: *I can't compete with a man in heels*

JASON: *Sorry I'm stuck at the office*

KATE: *(crying face emojis)*

JASON: *I have to put in some quality face-to-face with the new client. I'll get there as soon as I can*

KATE: *Well you have fun with your face-to-face. I'll have fun getting faceless*

Kate puts her phone away. She downs both orgasms.

KATE

Some of a girl's best times are on her own.

MUSIC/SONG: WE DANCED REPRISE

Kate, Stardust and Hot Waiter dance. Stardust sings parts of 'We Danced' as they dance, making fun of Frankie's moves and adding a few of her own. The impression is that Kate is having big party night and lots of drinking is happening. As they get rowdier and drunker they gradually go off.

END SONG

SCENE ENDS

SCENE FOUR - FRANKIE'S NIGHTCLUB, LATER THAT NIGHT

Frankie enters the empty stage and starts to clear away glasses – It's clearly after closing time and everyone has gone. Jason rushes in – he looks around, and is disappointed.

JASON

She's not here, is she?

FRANKIE

You've just missed her - she needs a good rest. She's going to do all my new costumes for Acapulco. You take all this for granted (indicates Jason's styled suit).

She does do you well, you know. Better than I used to do you in college, I hate to admit.

Stardust has entered during this and gasps as he thinks he's heard a bit of juicy gossip.

JASON

My suit, Stardust. Frankie thinks I take Kate's talents for granted.

STARDUST

Ha! You wouldn't be the only one. If a few more people around here started noticing what was right in front of them –

Stardust makes a face and exits. Frankie and Jason look at each other for a moment.

FRANKIE

Take a load off. It's been too long between drinks!

JASON

You're too busy with Kate - with FashionEsther - all the time. I never get to spend much time with either of you.

FRANKIE

Green doesn't suit you, Jason. You're my bud, Kate's my BFF.

JASON

I know it sounds stupid, but it's like Esther's taking over. All that bitchy stuff that Esther says? That stuff sounds more like something you'd say.

FRANKIE

I resent that remark. You know Kate loved designing, but she chose you and kids (and me). She's still got to channel that part of her somewhere - and enter FashionEsther! It's fabulous! Your wife has re-invented herself. Catch up! Spice it up! Write her some love letters.

JASON

Oh yeah? Dear Kate, get off your phone.

FRANKIE

Hmm, I don't think that'll work. Maybe take her dancing.

JASON

Dancing? Pfft. She's seen all my moves.

FRANKIE

Well let's see if we can't teach an old dog a new trick. I'll even let you lead. (they come into partner stance) Well look at you, aren't you a regular Fred.

JASON

Come on Ginger.

FRANKIE

Nice moves...perhaps all you needed was the right partner.

SONG: PENNED WITH INK

FRANKIE (singing)
A story in show-form told in song
Done the right way, can be lots of fun

JASON
See how Gen X can lose their way
Keeping up with the lingo of the day
Gen Y has it covered or so they think

JASON AND FRANKIE
Nothing says I love you more
Than when it's penned with ink
No, nothing says I love you more
Nothing says I love you more
Nothing says I love you more

Than when it's penned with ink.

END SONG

Frankie and Jason exit.

SCENE FIVE - KATE & JASON'S BEDROOM, THREE WEEKS LATER

Kate in her pyjamas, hair a mess. She's sketching designs on a large art pad. Surrounded by sketches/papers. A FaceChat call comes in on her phone from Gloria, and she has to search for her phone under the papers.

                    KATE
Hi, Ma.

            GLORIA (ON SCREEN)
Hello darling. Oooh. Late night?

                    KATE
Don't start, Ma.

            GLORIA (ON SCREEN)
I'm just saying that for a woman who loves to criticize other people's 'looks', well …

                    KATE
You call for a reason, Ma?

            GLORIA (ON SCREEN)
You really need to be a little kinder with these fashion types darling, you know how sensitive they can be.

                    KATE

What do you mean?

Gloria is obviously reading off her computer screen, next to the call window.

GLORIA (ON SCREEN)
"Rich in colour, beautiful flow, but it itched like a bitch all night." Not comments designed to make friends, Kate.

KATE
Esther is real, Ma, that's the point. She talks to real women who want to hear the truth.

GLORIA (ON SCREEN)
I'm simply saying that a little white lie hurts no-one. You need these designers to be on your side.

KATE
Like lying about your age, Ma?

GLORIA (ON SCREEN)
It's a jungle out there, Kate. You don't know what it's like.

KATE
It's better to just be yourself, surely.

GLORIA (ON SCREEN)
(snorts) Said no-one ever. I'm just saying you were nicer when you created fashion, rather than just commenting on it.

KATE
I can't believe you would say that! You have no filter.

GLORIA (ON SCREEN)

Look at your stories, Kate, neither do you.

They sit silent. In the background Kate can see her grandmother, NANNA, sleeping in an armchair.

KATE

Ma, what's wrong with Nanna? She's sleeping an awful lot lately.

GLORIA (ON SCREEN)

Well I have to run.

Gloria moves across the screen, trying to block Kate's view of Nanna.

KATE

Ma, you're scaring me. What's wrong with Nanna?

GLORIA (ON SCREEN)

Well, it's just a little mix up on my part really. By accident at first of course. So I've been giving her the nightly sedative in the morning instead of her vitamins. Here, look at the bottles, they're practically the same.

Gloria holds up two bottles that look completely different.

KATE

Ma, you gotta stop drugging Nanna!

GLORIA (ON SCREEN)

Don't you take that tone with me. Between your grandmother and you girls and your kids I get no time to myself. Just yesterday I had to rush over here, she thought she'd broken her hip. So I drive all the way over and turns out, she was wearing different shoes. One flat and one heel. All that panic for shoes Kate!

KATE

Ma!

GLORIA (ON SCREEN)

You'd better watch that temper. Frankie is right about you, you are a MILF!

KATE

Frankie? What are you talking about Mum?

GLORIA (ON SCREEN)

Menopause Is Looming Friend!

KATE

It's not what that means.

GLORIA (ON SCREEN)

Well, with your mood swings…

KATE

Of course you would just make up whatever suits you. But you gotta stop using LOL for lots of love. That funeral notice you put in for Vi - "Teddy will be sorely missed, LOL Gloria and the family".

GLORIA (ON SCREEN)

They charge by the letter Kate. I'm on a fixed income. Besides, he was a bit of a so and so…

GLORIA AND KATE

May he rest in peace. (cross themselves)

GLORIA (ON SCREEN)

Anyway, I've got to put my face on. I'm online with Brian in a minute.

KATE

Brian? I thought it was David?

GLORIA

Oh, David - the golfer. I had to ghost him. Not able to get a hole in one, if you know what I mean.

KATE

Too much information, Ma.

GLORIA

Love you darling. Gloria out!

Kate reflects. She begins to post.

ON SCREEN Social media posts from FashionEsther:

Too busy to talk – stay tuned Esties #milf #madfordrag #acapulcodreaming

Kate continues to draw. Facechat call from Cleo comes in.

Cleo is wearing her dance gear, stretching her arm along the length of her leg.

CLEO (ON SCREEN)

I hate working.

KATE

But it's good that you've got so many students, right?

CLEO (ON SCREEN)

Is it?

Cleo is horrified at this prospect. She continues her stretching and reaches off-screen, when she straightens up she has a glass of champagne in her hand.

CLEO (ON SCREEN)
I don't think I can do "poor" anymore.
I just had a half hour private but I let the poor girl out early.
Can you believe her Tiger mother was upset that I gave her kid an early mark? Who doesn't like an early mark?

KATE
On another note, Miss Poor-Uptown- Penthouse-with-a-nanny-and-kids-in- private-school – without tooting my own horn – beep beep – the costumes are done! Just in time, too. The boys fly out today.

CLEO (ON SCREEN)
Thank God Frankie saw sense and decided to take Stardust.
At least one of them will be dancing something resembling my choreography.

KATE
They really do make a perfect double act. (sighs)
It's meant some all-nighters, squeezing it all in between the kids and Jason, Ma, Nanna - and FashionEsther ... I'm actually shattered. But I really feel like my creative juices have been stimulated by this...actually, I just started to work on some -

CLEO (ON SCREEN)
At least one of us is being stimulated. Meanwhile I'm growing cobwebs. Working in a gay club has its downsides. (she has an idea)
Don't move, I'll be there in a second.
She grabs the whole champagne bottle and hangs ups. Moments later Cleo walks on stage with the champagne bottle.

KATE

That was fast.

CLEO

I've got a plan! We both need a holiday - let's follow Frankie to Acapulco! You should see the costumes in action anyway, and I should see how they butcher my choreography.

KATE

I can't just go! Jason, the kids.

CLEO

What about them? Jason will be fine. And Mum can help. She'll love it.

They both pause. And then laugh loudly together.

CLEO

Great! All sorted. I'll even help you pack. You won't know what to bring.

Cleo hands champagne to Kate and goes to Kate's wardrobe, pulls out a bag, and begins to sort through clothes. She pulls out two dresses, one is sexy, the other conservative.

CLEO

You'd pick "Hi Mum".

She holds up the conservative dress.

CLEO

But you need - "Hellooooo Mummy!"

Holding up the sexy dress. She tosses the conservative dress away and puts the other in the bag. Cleo continues to pick clothes and toss them in the suitcase.

KATE
What about your kids?

CLEO
Oh, they're away with Dr Dick and his foetus in some tropical Pacific Five-Star whatever!

KATE
Well, that's ...nice?

CLEO
He's just acclimatizing to the warm weather in preparation for his eternity in hell.
This is gonna be good. I can almost hear those steel drums now.

SONG: HOLIDAY - KATE AND CLEO

KATE
Staring at the window, virtual display
Million friends on Facepage
Haven't been out in days
Post-ing and Like-ing
I need to get away

CLEO
Rainy weather it doesn't bother me,
all my time in bed
Love me, shake me, move me,
take me all the way

KATE AND CLEO

Sea shells, by the sea shore
Sea shells by the sea shore

CLEO

Hmmm, Holiday J
umping Jack Flash
Feeling the sun down on my back
Taking it easy, just laying back
We need this time away
mmmm, Holiday

KATE AND CLEO

Ooooo, Holiday

Jason enters, home from work, sees the suitcase on the bed.

JASON

What's going on?

KATE

I'm thinking, it's not concrete… I'm going to Acapulco with Cleo
and Frankie. Are you good with that?
Should I go? I don't have to…

JASON

I think you should go.

KATE

Oh.

JASON

I think it would be good to have a break.

                              KATE
Oh, you think we need a break?

                             JASON
I think you need a break. You've been working really hard.

                              KATE
Well, you have too. All those late nights at the office. Why don't
you come too?

                             JASON
Kate, people with actual jobs can't just fly off at a moment's
notice.

Kate furious, grabs her bag and walks to the door.

                              KATE
Okay. Bye. Cleo, let's go.

Kate exits.

                             JASON
That's not what I meant.

                              CLEO
She'll be fine, she just needs a cocktail.

She grabs his hand and spins into him.

                              CLEO
Now don't miss me too much. We will pick up again when I get
back.

JASON

We'd better.

Cleo kisses him on the cheek, spins out and exits, Jason looks thoughtfully after her.

SCENE ENDS - BLACKOUT.

SCENE SIX - FRANKIE'S NIGHTCLUB, SHORTLY AFTER

Frankie enters with a suitcase, with Stardust close behind.

Stardust is dressed in safari gear with a bandanna around his head.

STARDUST

I've got my malaria tablets, I've got my mosquito net. I've got my first aid kit, electrolytes, protein bars. I've got my activated charcoal, my probiotics, my wet wipes. Costumes all packed right here. (pats the suitcases. Points to his head) And, bandannas, of course.

FRANKIE

That's all well and good, Stardust, but nothing's going to save you when you got no shame. It's a cabaret show, not a safari.

STARDUST

I just don't want anything to go wrong. Not now that I'm indispensable.

Kate and Cleo enter, carrying suitcases.

CLEO

We're coming to Acapulco!

FRANKIE

Kate! That's great! Stardust, you're off costumes.

STARDUST

They're pressed, packed and tissued. What else is there to do?

KATE

Thankyou darling. Now you can just concentrate on your performance.

Stardust is mollified. He turns to Cleo excitedly.

CLEO AND STARDUST

Girls weekend!

KATE

Actually I am a bit excited. I can't remember the last time I went away on my own. (the others look at her, like, what are we?) I mean without the kids. And Jason.

FRANKIE

Jason's not coming?

KATE

Nope. He's "working". (she pulls herself up from being nasty) Actually he has been working back a lot lately. And I think he's been working out - there's a lot of extra active wear in the wash. And I keep catching him looking at himself in the mirror, sucking his stomach in. To be honest, it's been a bit weird.

CLEO

Maybe he's got another woman!

STARDUST

It's as plain as all the noses that have been on her face (points at Cleo)! He's having a midlife crisis.

SONG: MIDLIFE CRISIS

Frankie, Stardust, Cleo and Kate

(Note: Kate and Frankie are singing about Jason, Cleo about Richard, Stardust about Frankie)

STARDUST *(singing)*

He's having a mid-life crisis
His got his fingers up in the air
Sitting at a funky café
Shame he got no hair

FRANKIE

Pulling up outside the club
In his flash new car
Waiting at the bar for service
But he's waving his seniors card

STARDUST AND FRANKIE

He's having a midlife crisis
Plain as it can be
Having a mid-life crisis
That's what it looks like…
Looks like to me

CLEO

Online upgrading models
Trying to change his life
Cut to the chase all he's after
Is a brand-new trophy wife

It's so obvious
Changing cologne, Shaving his body Spending money like it's loose
change
You're loving yourself
Your selfish self's on the brain

CLEO AND KATE

He's having a midlife crisis
He's having a midlife crisis
Plain as it can be
Having a mid-life crisis
That's what it looks like...
Looks like to me

KATE

Looks like to me
Loving yourself
Your selfish self's on the brain
It's so insane
It's so insane
Your selfish self's on the brain

As the song is ending they are all collecting their bags and dance off.
The costume cases are left, forgotten in the middle of the stage.

END SCENE – BLACKOUT

SCENE CHANGE - ON SCREEN Social media posts from
FashionEsther:

Headfirst into holidays #cliffhanger #acapulcobaby #milfontour,

Threads, Feathers, Flying high #cloudsofcolour,

Touchdown #cocktailtime #milfontour

SCENE SEVEN - ACAPULCO NIGHTCLUB, THEN RESORT BEDROOM

Kate and Cleo are in the Acapulco burlesque nightclub. Cleo is in cougar-mode. Kate is overwhelmed. The waitress, BANJO, circles around. There is a young man, BRAD, ordering a drink. (Other Actors may be included as other club patrons.)

KATE
Ma was right - it <u>is</u> a jungle out here.

CLEO
And the lion won't be sleeping tonight.

KATE
These all look like they could be my kid's friends. In fact, I'm pretty sure that one's had a sleep- over at our house.

CLEO
How many rips do you think he's got in those jeans?

KATE
Eight. I thought Frankie and Stardust would already be here.

Cleo grabs a menu as Banjo passes by.

CLEO
You know what gay men are like. They have their own time zone. They'll be home with cucumbers – beauty sleep. They won't be any fun until after they've done the show tomorrow night.
(reading the menu) Fluffy duck, Black Russian - oh, listen to this one - Caribbean Queen.

Kate runs her finger down the menu.

CLEO

You want a Cherry Sundae?

KATE

Yes, but obviously they don't have them.

CLEO

Yes they do.

Cleo grabs Banjo who is walking past, takes the order pad and begins to write.

CLEO

Here, this will be the best cocktail you'll ever make. Start us off with four.

She hands the pad back with a wink. She takes her Amex gold card from her cleavage and slips it seductively into Banjo's pocket.

KATE

Dick's card?

CLEO

Of course darling. He would want it that way. (to Banjo) Run along gorgeous.

KATE

I can't wait, I haven't had a Cherry Sundae since...

CLEO

Since you were busy losing your...

They both laugh, remembering. Cleo's phone pings.

CLEO

Ah, a text from my darlings. (She reads). Right, I see.
The "foetus" has a new string of pearls, the children have been
doing scenic tours in a helicopter all afternoon, and they've
enjoyed jet-skiing so much that Dr Dick's bought them two jet-
ski's to bring home.
Well clearly, Dr Dick hasn't thought that one through.
Guess who's getting a brand new waterfront home!
She gets a pearl necklace, I get the crown jewels!
(She calls out to the whole club) Cherry Sundaes for everybody!!!
Cos Dr Dick would want it that way!

Cleo grabs BRAD and begins to sing. During the song Banjo brings a
jug of cocktail and two glasses to Kate. During the song Cleo switches
attention from Brad to Banjo.

SONG: SPOONFUL

CLEO (singing burlesque style)
You're cooking tonight,
We've got the candlelight.
Now you tell me you're through,
If you can't give me love,
I'll take a spoonful.

ENSEMBLE
Oh, ah etc spoonful

CLEO
If you can't commit,
I'll stuff it in my pocket,
I'll wait a bit.
I'll wait for the rest of my life,

Drop some love in a cup,
I'll eat it all up.

Tell me it's true,
I'll take your love, by the spoonful.
You got the right recipe,
A spoonful is all that I need.

Cleo is engaging Kate in the song.

CLEO
You're like hot chocolate,
When I get close, you make me melt.
I thought you felt it too,
Just give it up, and take a spoonful.

I saw you tonight,
Cooking something special, is it mine?
Give me some sort of a sign,
Dip it in your sugar,
I'll eat it all up.

CLEO AND KATE
Tell me is it true,
I'll take your love, by the spoonful.
You got the right recipe,
A spoonful is all that I need.

CLEO
Pour your love on me,
I like the way you make me feel

KATE
Sugar and honey,

I wanna taste, the fantasy

I'll take your love, by the spoonful.
You got the right recipe,
A spoonful is all that I, all that I need.

KATE AND CLEO
Tell me is it true,
I'll take your love, by the spoonful.
You got the right recipe,
A spoonful is all I need

KATE
A spoonful is all that I need

CLEO
A spoonful is all that I need.

END SONG

Cleo exits with Banjo, giving Kate a little wave. Kate has finished the song in the arms of Brad, and she's now a little flustered.

BRAD
Well hi. You come here often?

KATE
Do you mean Acapulco? (awkward pause)
How long have you been alive? I mean, how long ago did you arrive?

BRAD
I live here.
I'm in my gap year helping build houses for the poor.

KATE

Oh God. Of course you are.

Kate goes to drink her cocktail, but puts the straw in the jug instead and drinks from that.

BRAD

I'm Brad.

KATE

That's a nice name.

BRAD

If you like the sound of that, you should hear my number.

KATE

Uh huh. You know, you kind of remind me of someone… never mind. I'm… Esther.

BRAD

Will your friend be alright?

KATE

My sister? She'll be fine.

Kate now notices that Cleo has left her phone on the table.

KATE

Oh Cleo! You've left your … never mind.

As Kate puts the phone back on the table, a message comes through from Jason. Kate looks and reads out loud. (message appears on screen)

KATE

"Turns out it does take two to tango. Can't do this without you.
Call me please LOL."
LOL??????

Kate is stunned and upset. The nightclub fades into darkness.

SONG: WOMAN

KATE (singing)
Looking into the darkness,
all alone with my soul
Now feeling like the fool
Everything I've known, now not true
Now I'm standing here feeling blue
Woman this shouldn't be happening to you

Woman, why do we hurt each other?
They play us off, play us off, like the fool
If you're the one now, just remember,
next time it might be you

Don't let the weight of the world fall on your shoulders,
and to yourself, to yourself always be true
Your heart will find the answer
Yeah, let love let love come to you, you , you

Woman, why do we hurt each other?
They play us off, play us off, like the fool
If you're the one now, just remember,
next time it might be you

Woman, why do we hurt each other?

They play us off, play us off, like the fool
If you're the one now,
If you're the one now,
next time it might be you

END SONG

Kate turns to Brad.

KATE
I don't think I can stay.

BRAD
No, me either. I'll be heading home at the end of the year.

KATE
No, no. I meant I need to be somewhere quieter. (she hesitates)
Would you like to …

BRAD
Sure.

The pair head out of the nightclub. Kate and Brad outside under big moon. Brad puts his arms around Kate and she gets spooked.

KATE
Sorry, this just isn't me.

Brad kisses her hand.

BRAD
Don't you think a moon like that deserves some attention?
Stay, Esther.

SONG: STAY

During the song they make their way Kate's resort bedroom.

KATE (singing)
Thank god I made it home before it got late
Just be quiet as you shut the gate.
Now I creep up the stairs
Somehow I think you don't really care

Love is like a roller coaster,
up and down the tracks
Who knows how fast it's going
Who knows how long it will last

When the moon is glowing in the night,
and the stars are shinning down so bright.
You said stay
You said stay
Could I stay?

Different seasons, their changes,
they're hot, cool, then cold
Is this how our love is going?
Has this love grown too old?

Don't let it stray, don't let it drift away again
Take these hands of mine,
let's go back in time
let's go back in time

When the moon is glowing in the night
When the stars are shining down so bright
You said stay
He said stay

Could I stay?

END SONG

As Kate sings, she and Brad dance their way in the moonlight back to her hut. While she sings, he also looks at his phone, takes some selfies etc. He's a bit impatient with her singing.

After the song ends, Kate and Brad are at the room. Kate wants the lights out and claps twice at the light to turn them off. Brad wants to see her in the light and claps the lights twice to turn them on. Kate slaps his bottom twice to turn them back off.

Lights go on and off, on and off, until all is quiet. Single tight spot on Kate:

KATE

What happens in Acapulco, stays in Acapulco, right?

END SCENE: BLACKOUT

SCENE CHANGE - ON SCREEN Social media posts from FashionEsther:

Day of reckoning #youcantsaynoinacapulco, #lookoutworld

SCENE EIGHT - RESORT BEDROOM, ACAPULCO, NEXT MORNING

Kate is asleep in the bed, there is a suspicious lump in the bed next to her (maybe Brad?). Jason bursts through the door, and Kate sits up, dressed in underwear. Jason launches into a rehearsed speech that peters out by the end.

JASON

So I was thinking that of course I could work online that's the one good thing to come out of Covid, and there are many actual real jobs that happen only in the online world, like yours, of course, and I why would I ever pass up a chance to be in Acapulco with you, because you and me is the most important thing there is, you can't do it all alone it takes two. Say something.

KATE

Two to tango?

Cleo sashays in through the door, she doesn't see Jason behind the open door.

CLEO

Who was a bad girl last night?

Cleo looks at the clothes strewn all over the floor and Kate in her underwear.

CLEO

I was talking about me... but do tell! (she sees lump in bed and points) Ooh ah! (whispering) Is that him?

JASON

Is that who?

CLEO

Ahh! Ooh ah...

KATE

How long has it been going on? My husband and my own sister.

Banjo enters through the door.

BANJO

You've been sleeping with your sister's husband?

CLEO

What? No, ewwwww.

KATE

Don't try to deny –

Frankie enters in high drama.

FRANKIE

I'm ruined! I'm ruined! The costumes, Kate. We've got no costumes!

KATE

Wait, what?

FRANKIE

I'm a drag queen with nothing to wear. Inconceivable!

Stardust enters, sauntering.

STARDUST

"You're off costumes, Stardust." Good decision. Where are the costumes, Kate? Back at the club, Kate?

KATE

Oh my god. The cases.

JASON

Is this really the biggest problem here?

Frankie insulted, gasps.

KATE

No, it isn't. (Frankie gasps again) The biggest problem is that the two people I trust most in the world have screwed me over, literally.

CLEO

What? Kate, it was all for you!

KATE

Enough. Here's your phone Cleo. I saw your message, Jason. "Can't do this without you".

CLEO

The tango Kate, I've been teaching Jason the tango.

JASON

Because Frankie told me to spice things up. To re-invent myself. For you.

STARDUST

Another good idea from Frankie!

CLEO

(to Banjo) I would never, ever sleep with him.

KATE

The tango? Oh. I thought, I thought... Oh.

FRANKIE

Kate, is there someone in the bed with you?

Everyone looks at the lump. Kate is frozen, rabbit in the headlights.

JASON

Kate?

When Kate doesn't move, Jason flings the covers back to reveal pillows bunched up.

KATE
I made them Jason-shaped. I missed you.

She holds out her hand to him and he pulls her into a tango hold, and begins to sing and dance the tango. Frankie & Stardust, Cleo & Banjo pair up to dance.

SONG: THE BOMB

JASON
It was a hot long night, when we had that fight
I knew our love was strong,
after the fight we had that night
I knew I couldn't be wrong
Talk to me, talk to me
cause you're the only one
Don't you know, don't you, don't you know

Baby you're the bomb
cause you turn me on,
cause you turn me oo-on
Come to me, come to me
cause you're the only one

Don't you know, don't you know, don't you know
Baby you're the bomb
cause you turn me on,
cause you turn me oo-on
Come to me, come to me
cause you're the only one

Don't you know, don't you know, don't you know

Whoa whoa etc
You're the one, you're the one
So baby don't you run
You're the one, you're the one
So baby don't you run
You're the one, you're the one
So baby don't you run
You're the one, you're the one

Baby, you're the bomb
cause you turn me on,
cause you turn me oo-on
Come to me, come to me
cause you're the only one
Don't you know, don't you know, don't you know
Baby you're the Bomb

END SONG

Song finishes. Each couple kisses. Frankie and Stardust are mesmerised by each other (their first kiss). Banjo's comment snaps them back to the present.

BANJO
So what about the costumes?

STARDUST
The housekeeping girl makes a good point. Actually I need some clean towels in 105 when you're done here.

CLEO
Everyone, this is Banjo. (she kisses Banjo)

EVERYONE ELSE
Hiiiiii Banjo.

FRANKIE
Kate, what are we going to do about the costumes?

STARDUST
That you left behind. Pressed, packed and tissued.

FRANKIE
We're on stage in 8 hours.

Kate looks around the room, notes Banjo's work shirt and bedspread are same hotel motif fabric.

KATE
I think I've got an idea. Banjo, can you rustle up some old work uniforms? And bedspreads?

BANJO
Sure thing.

KATE
Jason, I need to you find me a sewing machine. Frankie, you're on shoes. Stardust - velcro, thread, feathers, wigs, sparkles and a glue gun.

STARDUST
Consider it done.

FRANKIE
(to Stardust) Indispensable! Wardrobe improvisation is one of my favourite things!

                            KATE
Go!

All exit except Kate and Cleo.

                            CLEO
OK, dish. I saw you MILFing with that backpacker, hmm?
Momma's inner loins flaring?

                            KATE
Might intentionally, like, forget.

                            CLEO
More info lady friend.

                            KATE
Mind is little fuzzy.

                            CLEO
Maybe ingest latte frappe?

                            KATE
Might indulge large fries.

They laugh but that hurts Kate's head.

                            KATE
Ohhhhh, those Cherry Sundays! Takes me back to 18. All I
needed after a big night was a can of coke and cold pizza.

                            CLEO
Mmm, and a pack of ciggie's (aside) and a pregnancy test.
(to Kate) Remember when everything was that simple?

SONG: CHERRY SUNDAY

KATE

Cherry Sunday on my side
Bluer Monday catch a ride
Season pass to the sun
I got my radar programmed for fun
Dah, dah, dah (etc), ooo

CLEO

Feel like a dreamer chasing the stars
I'd like to visit Venus or Mars
Rainbow chaser is how I feel
Think I'll go fishing, throw me a reel
Dah, dah, dah etc

KATE AND CLEO

You by my side, makes me feel so right
You by my side, makes me feel so right
You by my side, makes me feel so right

END SONG

Kate and Cleo hug.

KATE

I love us.

CLEO

If we're going to do this, we need coffee.

KATE

I'd just better check on the kids – I'm calling Ma.

CLEO

Whoa ok, you're on your own with that one. Say hi.

Cleo exits. Kate makes a Facechat call to Gloria. Nanna answers.

NANNA (ON SCREEN)

Kate, darling! When are you coming home? The kids are lovely, fine, wonderful … but that boy of yours is never off the Xbox and it's not that I mind at all, it's your mother, yesterday she missed Antiques Roadshow and you know she never misses Antiques Roadshow, and I don't think the kids realized but I could tell she was upset.

Nanna inclines her head, indicating Gloria fast asleep in the chair in background.

KATE

Hi Nanna. Why is Ma asleep at this time of day?

NANNA (ON SCREEN)

Oh, she's been burning the candle at both ends from what I've gathered, with, oh I don't know,
Brian, I think his name is … and this David fellow keeps calling and I don't know what to tell him. I've put the phone on silent. I think she needs a break.

KATE

Oh, Nanna. I've really messed things up, and now I've got to fix it all, and I don't know if I can do it.

NANNA (ON SCREEN)

Darling, it's the screwups that make us stronger. You'll be fine. Not fine - you'll be fabulous.
You're a MILF, after all. Mastering irritating life fuckups.

KATE

Thanks Nanna.

(phone vibrating sounds)

NANNA (ON SCREEN)

Oh for god's sake here's another one! Rajesh. Honestly. I've gotta go. Swipe right my arse.

She hangs up. Pause where Kate reflects.

KATE

(sings acapella) Well, I never said that I was per-er-erfect.

SONG: MY SONG

Kate in spot. Behind her stage is changed to Acapulco Nightclub.

KATE

I'm making creating
no longer faking
I'm finally singing MY song
Just scratch the surface
Everybody needs purpose
A place that you really belong
Oh oh oh oh
My Song

END SONG

Cleo rushes on stage, she's dressed up, carrying a dress and shoes.

CLEO

Kate, here it is. Hurry! It's time. The Guy is waiting. We've got to get out there.

KATE

Already! (to audience) It's like no time has passed at all.

Kate dresses on stage with Cleo's help.

CLEO

I can't believe you did it, you're truly amazing.

KATE

We all did it together.

CLEO

All is a big word, Kate. But we've done what we can do, now it's up to Frankenstein and his Bride to pull it off.

Music starts (Stronger). Jason comes on to join Kate and Cleo. They wait but there's no appearance. Then Banjo rushes over to them and music stops.

BANJO

There's been a glue gun incident! (to audience) Is there anybody with arts and crafts experience?
Scrapbooker? Is that even a thing anymore?
Nevermind. We just need two minutes.

Everyone freezes in panic as Banjo rushes off. Jason steps up to fill the gap, thinking on his feet.

JASON

A big hand for FashionEsther, who created everything you're going to see tonight, and would like to say a few words to introduce the show. Give it up for FashionEsther, our favourite

MILF!

Kate horrified, takes to the stage. Jason is gesturing 'sorry, I panicked'.
She stumbles up and starts talking nervously. As she goes on she gains
momentum.

KATE
Thank you, Jason. Typical women being late, right. (pathetic
laugh) So, I'm FashionEsther...

VOICE FROM OFFSTAGE
MILF woooo!

KATE
Oh uh, yeah... MILF. I mean, like what??? So strange. Like...
"Mother I'd Like to literally... Follow home and have sex with"
ha ha ha... But that's not totally bad right? We can own it, right
girls? We're like, I want the job, equality, respect, but if we get
called a MILF we're still like "Yes I am".
But not all the time. Here's a tip – If your woman says 'could you
ever put the toilet seat down' or 'empty the dishwasher' if you say
honey you're such a MILF, she's not going to say that's okay you
go get yourself a beer, I've got this.
She's going to look at you from the sink while washing those last
few dishes by hand and a hot flash will literally set her body on
fire and she'll be thinking MILF? Menopause is literally fu...
fu... fairly unpleasant.

There's dead silence. Cleo begins to clap and encourage audience to
clap and cheer. Kate smiles shakily. Music starts again and Frankie and
Stardust enter in full drag costumes, with resort motif fabric prominent.

SONG: STRONGER STRONGER

FRANKIE

You got a beautiful energy
I feel it all around me,
won't you take me to the place your heart is in
(Ensemble: your heart is in)

KATE

Life has so many splendours
In your arms I am rendered
I want to be in a world you live in
(Ensemble: you live in)

WHOLE CAST

Energy is the power you feel in me
Can you see it, come on now believe in me
You can see that this isn't wrong now
Only you can make me feel stronger

KATE AND CLEO

Stronger
Stronger Stronger
Stronger Stronger

STARDUST

(Spoken/rap)
You're the one I'll run to baby
Come to me and don't say maybe
I can't wait a minute longer
You're the one that makes me stronger
Feel the shivers down my spine
Thought of you boy, you're divine
Feel your sweat you know I'm gonna

You're the one that makes me stronger

KATE AND CLEO

Stronger
Stronger Stronger
Stronger Stronger
Stronger Stronger

WHOLE CAST

Energy is the power you feel in me
Can't you see it, Come on now, believe in me
You can see that this isn't wrong now
Only you can make me feel stronger

KATE AND CLEO

Stronger
Stronger Stronger
Stronger Stronger

CLEO

You got a beautiful harmony
I feel eternally happy
I wanna fly to the sky and be free

JASON

Life has so many colors,
Look around at all the wonders
I wanna be a part of every living thing

KATE

Energy is the power you feel in me
Can't you see it, come on now believe in me
You can see that this isn't wrong now
Only you can make me feel stronger

WHOLE CAST
Energy is the power you feel in me
Can't you see it, come on now believe in me
You can see that this isn't wrong now
Only you can make me feel stronger

Stronger

Stronger music repeats as cast begin bows but is interrupted when Frankie gets a Facechat call from THE GUY. Everyone gets excited.

FRANKIE
It's The Guy! It's the Guy!

Ad lib - everyone gets excited but Frankie shushes them (including audience) and answers call.

THE GUY (ON SCREEN)
Love you. Love the show. Love the costumes. I want all of you. The complicated MILF as well. It will be a hit. My people will be in touch.

GLORIA (ON SCREEN)
(leans in to the call) Hi Darling! Isn't it exciting? David loves you.

KATE
Ma? What are you doing?

GLORIA (ON SCREEN)
You know, the guy I've been telling you about? David! He plays Golf.

Music starts. ENCORE AND BOWS – Stronger, whole cast. On screen characters can do bows and dance on screen.

ON SCREEN

#MILF LOGO

THE END

ABOUT THE AUTHOR

Sally Knight, was born in Melbourne, Victoria, Australia, on November 05, 1968,

Sally's passion for music and the stage has driven her career across various fields, including writing, singing, and performing in musical theatre.

MILF The Musical reflects Sally's vibrant personality and life experiences, in addition to her musical pursuits, Sally has applied her creativity to the commercial radio industry, crafting copy for prominent global brands.

The musical, initially performed at the Historic Avoca Beach Theatre, received enthusiastic reviews in "Stage Whispers" prompting Sally to take her work to New York, off-Broadway to The Theatre Centre where Catherine Russell Star of Perfect Crime, did a quest reading in *MILF* as Kate's colourful mother Gloria.

In New York, *MILF* has been met with widespread acclaim, and Sally is preparing for a pivotal moment that represents a significant and daring step in her career as she continues to take risks and embrace new opportunities.

Her diverse talents and experiences have culminated in *MILF* a musical celebrated for its relatable themes, colourful characters, and original music.

ORiGiN™
Theatrical

FOR ALL ENQUIRIES CONTACT:
ORiGiN™ Theatrical
PO BOX Q1235, QVB Post Office, Sydney, NSW, 1230, Australia
Phone: (61 2) 8514 5201
enquiries@originmusic.com.au   www.origintheatrical.com.au
Part of the ORiGiN™ Music Group
An Australian Independent Music Company